THROUGH
THE EYES OF A
STORM

T0158754

THROUGH
THE EYES OF A
STORM

PERSPECTIVE GAINED THROUGH
A CANCER JOURNEY

MARK A. MCSWAIN

iUniverse, Inc.
Bloomington

Through the Eyes of a Storm
Perspective Gained through a Cancer Journey

iUniverse books may be ordered through booksellers or by contacting:

iUniverse
1663 Liberty Drive
Bloomington, IN 47403
www.iuniverse.com
1-800-Authors (1-800-288-4677)

ISBN: 978-1-4620-3192-4 (sc)
ISBN: 978-1-4620-3193-1 (ebk)

Printed in the United States of America

iUniverse rev. date: 07/23/2011

CONTENTS

THROUGH THE EYES OF A STORM

Perspective Gained Through a Cancer Journey

This book is dedicated to my loving wife
and faithful caregiver, Dottie, and to our
sons, Scott and Matthew.

Written in honor of the countless souls who
have journeyed through cancer or who are
currently in the midst of the storm.

SPECIAL ACKNOWLEDGMENT

I want to acknowledge the amazing medical care I have been blessed with. While I acknowledge God as the Great Physician, He placed some wonderful people in my life, and Dottie and I cannot imagine this journey without them. I will speak of some specific people in the pages ahead. Words cannot express my thanks for the genuine concern and outstanding care given me by Drs. Read, Kirkland, Reese, Georgiou, and Gilbert.

I could not have endured the journey without my church family. They will be mentioned at times in the following pages. John Norvell and Matthew Mincher, our associate minister and student minister, respectively, buoyed me up during the most difficult time in my life. They took care of our church family, and for that I will forever be grateful.

The staff at Henry Joyce Cancer Clinic was phenomenal. Their sweet smiles, authentic concern, and patience set me at ease during very anxious times. To the chemo lab nurses at Vanderbilt and the Jackson Clinic, I do not have the vocabulary to express to you what I feel for you. You are a special group of angels. Thank you from the bottom of my heart, and God bless you all!

Dr. Netterville, my ENT at Vanderbilt, you and your staff have encouraged me, answered my frantic questions, reassured me, while being very candid about my condition. Georgette, you in particular have been a blessing beyond words. Thanks for the pizza recommendation!

Dr. Georgiou and the entire staff at the Kirkland Cancer Center, currently located in the Jackson Madison County General Hospital, have continued to be an encouragement to me. Thank you not only for the work you do but for the fact you go about it as a ministry to others. You are a blessing! Dr. Georgiou, I look forward to that cup of coffee on my 90th birthday. Thank you for your friendship. But, I really look forward to the day you are without a job or have to change professions!

INTRODUCTION

We are very familiar with storms. With modern technology, forecasters are often able to predict storm development, severity, and direction. With that information, forecasters are able to issue warnings. People in the storm's path have time to prepare, perhaps lessening the effect of the storm. At other times, storms hit unexpectedly leaving shock, dismay, shattered lives, and destruction in their wakes.

Recently, a cyclone Myanmar took the lives of many and left untold destruction. Each year, typhoons and hurricanes churn their way through islands and coast lines leaving unimaginable destruction in their wake. Citizens in the central United States experience the fear and devastation left from tornados. On February 9, 2008, an enormous and powerful tornado hit particularly close to home for our family. Our eldest son, Scott, was a student at Union University in Jackson Tennessee. The F4 tornado that hit the campus that evening destroyed much of the campus including the majority of student housing. Our son was in one of the dormitories.

Uncertainty, concern, fear, and panic filled our hearts as we sought to hear from our son and the other students on the campus. When I arrived on the campus that night, I found a frightening scene, with students surrounded by darkness and destruction. Darkness and destruction are characteristic of the nature of storms. However, much can be learned from storms. From the rubble, life lessons can arise that might not be learned apart from the storm.

While one might never face a tornado, cyclone, hurricane, or typhoon, very few of us make it through life without crises or troubling times. These storms of life are indiscriminant. They hit the wealthy and the poor, the young and the old. These ominous, life changing events leave hurt, destruction, confusion, isolation, and other such rubble in their paths. All of which can lead to hopelessness, making the possibility of recovery unimaginable.

The president of Union University, Dr. David Dockery, said of the 2008 tornado:

We moved from this unforgettable event with hope. Hope is a powerful word—a driving force in life. Hope includes a desire for something, but it is even more than that. It is an eager, confident expectation that sustains us while we work diligently and wait patiently. Hope is not escapism, but is an energizing motivation for faithful living in the here and now. In the midst of life's challenges and struggles, hope stabilizes our lives, serving as an anchor to link us to God's faithfulness. Hope shares and directs our service and gives it motivation so that while we wait and watch, we work faithfully.[1]

My hope and prayer for this little book is that it will bring a word of hope to someone in the midst of one of life's storms, or, who is experiencing the darkness and destruction of the aftermath. I hope, just as Dr. Dockery said, someone might be encouraged to find the motivation to LIVE in the here and now even while they are in the midst of the most challenging situation of their lives. Further, I hope they might find the energy to faithfully carry on living as they watch and wait for what the Father has in store for them.

A word from Scripture is in order before we proceed. Jesus gathered his disciples together following a long day of teaching. Boarding a boat, the Lord and his disciples began a journey across the Sea of Galilee. As often happens on that particular body of water, a furious squall came upon them. It was a storm that brought great fear to the most hardened fishermen present. In fact, they called for the Lord, who had fallen asleep in the stern of the boat, and asked him, "don't you care if we drown?"

The answer is yes, He cared. He used the situation to teach them a great lesson they would have not learned otherwise. He taught them to trust him. Oh, by the way, after the storm, the situation

---

[1] David Dockery, Unionite Special Edition 2008, vol. 59, number 2, pg. 3.

is described as completely calm! We need to know, as believers, calm is coming. The storm will not last forever. In fact, by its nature, a storm cannot last forever!

This book was written from the perspective of a cancer patient. People have used a number of terms to put some perspective on cancer. It has been called a fight or a battle. I have chosen to call it a journey. You will see that term throughout this book.

Finally, my storm was cancer. Your storm may be something totally different. I believe the things I share in this book can be beneficial as you journey through any storm. God bless you as you read and as you journey.

CHAPTER 1

THE DARKNESS OF THE HOUR

**"We are hard pressed on every
side, but not crushed; perplexed,
but not in despair; persecuted,
but not abandoned; struck down,
but not destroyed."
2 Cor 4:8-9 (NIV)**

Certainly suffering has been a part of man's existence since the first man and woman were expelled from the Garden of Eden. It may appear our suffering, our storm, is much worse than the storms of others. I do not in any way want to insinuate my storm was unique in its power. I simply share some of the details as a testimony to the grace of God and to show that you and I might have some common bond.

Perhaps you have heard the story of Job. He lost his children, his livestock, and his health. On top of the heavy losses, he was nagged by his wife and friends. In the midst of this storm, Job quickly got to the point he declared, "If only I had never come into being, or had been carried straight from the womb to the grave! Are not my few days almost over? Turn away from me so I can have a moment's joy before I go to the place of no return, to the land of gloom and deep shadow, to the land of deepest night, of deep shadow and disorder, where even the light is like darkness."(Job 10.18-22, NIV)

If Job and the psalmists, along with many of the Bible's characters, experienced despair and depression in the midst of the darkness of life's storms, we, too, are subject to those overwhelming feelings. We must determine, by the grace of God, not to stay in the grip of despair.

My storm began with an early warning sign. Prior to leaving on vacation, I dropped by the clinic to get some cold symptoms checked out. During the exam the doctor discovered an enlarged lymph node. While he was not overly concerned and said it was probably nothing to worry about, he said I should follow up with my personal physician when we return from our trip.

These were the initial winds. They appeared to be insignificant. However, looking back, they were the initial storm front making its presence known.

The following months consisted of being passed from one doctor to another. I had some dental issues that culminated in a root canal. The enlarged node was just below the tooth involved. All of my doctors agreed that the issue was more than likely related to lingering infection. The course of treatment was antibiotics. The node would respond by reducing; the antibiotic would run its course and the node would remain. This routine went on for months. In fact, it went on until December 12, 2007. That was the day my life really took a scary turn and we entered the full brunt of the storm.

My ENT was doing a follow up exam. While feeling the base of my gum near where the tooth in question had now been removed, he found something. I saw his visage change and he sat down in front of me. I will never forget his words, "I feel a thickness that I have not felt before at the base of your tongue." He had bumped into it with the back of his finger. He said it felt smooth and symmetrical and it was more than likely something benign.

Nevertheless, he moved quickly. He sent me for the first of what would become many CT scans. On Thursday, the following day, he called me with the preliminary results. It still appeared to him that it was something benign. The specialists in Cleveland, Ohio, however, disagreed. Upon further consultation, consensus was that I had cancer. Friday morning Dottie and I went to Jackson Madison County General Hospital for a biopsy that would refute or confirm their diagnosis as well as determine what kind of cancer we were dealing with.

On Saturday morning the word came that it was indeed malignant. We had to wait until Monday for the exact diagnosis. Dottie's mom and dad along with my mom and step-dad came to our house that day so that we could break the news to them. Telling your loved ones that you have cancer is a very difficult thing. The hurt on their faces and the helpless despair was tough to handle. I wanted to tell them it was going to be alright. But I could not.

Monday came. A new week had begun. Would this be the beginning of a much better week than last? We thought it could not get any worse. But, it did. The storm seemed to grow out of control. We got word that the diagnosis was squama cell carsinoma. We were hopeful when we found out that it was a treatable cancer that often responded well to radiation and chemotherapy.

On Tuesday we found ourselves facing the unthinkable. The week before Christmas, the day after finding out the type of cancer I had, we got a devastating telephone call. I had just gotten to the office and was sitting in our secretary's office. I told our staff that God had blessed us with a good prognosis. We had a chance, a good chance. The words I spoke next turned out to be more prophetic than I ever intended. I told my staff that God had given us hope. I had a treatable cancer. I further said, "there will be people who will go to work today and not come home."

Upon leaving that office, I made my way down the hall to my study, taking out my keys to the door, I felt my phone vibrate in my pocket. Dottie told me that there had been an accident at the mill where her dad worked and that he had been injured. She did not know anything else but that we needed to make the seventy mile trip to the hospital. Once again my phone rang about half way through my trip across town to pick up Dottie. This time it was her brother. The shock and panic in his voice told the story. Their dad had been killed in the freak accident. Now, I had to deliver more devastating news to my wife and children.

God's hands of comfort and strength provided the only hope for Virginia, Lonnie, Gary, Dana (Dottie's mother and siblings), Dottie, and our families. Following the funeral, Dottie and I began weekly trips to Vanderbilt for chemotherapy treatments followed by more chemo and radiation nearer our home in Jackson, Tennessee. I lost my voice for a few weeks. Eating and drinking became very difficult and painful. Significant weight loss, infections, fatigue, uncertainty, radiation burn, a mouth filled with sores and all sorts of other issues were part of the battle. Through it all God's grace sustained us.

As I said earlier, I know there are many people who have suffered far more than I. Perhaps **you** have. Perhaps you are somewhere in the midst of a storm of some type right now. Maybe it is cancer, maybe it is another type of crisis. I pray, as you read these words, you will feel the warming and soothing touch of God. I hope that you will experience the peace that comes from knowing He will see you through the difficulties life often presents. I pray somewhere in the pages to follow, you find comfort and encouragement.

CHAPTER 2

GOD'S GRACE IS ENOUGH

**But he said to me, "My grace is
sufficient for you, for my power
is made perfect in weakness."
Therefore I will boast all the
more gladly about my
weaknesses, so that
Christ's power
may rest on me.
2 Cor 12:9 (NIV)**

My journey with and through cancer became a
journey of discovery. It was a journey physically,
spiritually, and emotionally. Every day was a
learning experience. I discovered a number of things
that helped me take the next step. Steps are often
difficult, but God has not left us to our own wisdom
and power. Over the first few weeks of treatment, I
searched feverishly through God's Word.

Remember at this point I was thinking, "I'm 44 years old and I love life . . . I love my life . . . I want to see my kids married and I want to hold my grandkids . . ." So, when I heard I had cancer, all sorts of things flashed through my mind. Some of those things took up residence. I guess that is human nature. We tend to worry. I did. We tend to dwell on the "what ifs." I did. We may even wonder if the fight is worth the effort. I did.

I began to search scripture for promises from God that I would live a long life, that He would heal me. I looked and looked. I found principles and promises of all kinds, but I did not find anything that promised me I would be healed. I found many instances that declare and demonstrate that He can. Indeed, I found a number of things in my search, and those are the things that I want to share with you.

But where do I start? What order do I place them in? What do I share and what do I leave out? There can be no better place to start than the grace of God.

It is amazing that you can hear about God's grace all of your life; teach it; preach it; and, know that it is enough for any situation. Then, when the unthinkable arises, you begin to wonder and even perhaps doubt if you have the strength to take another step, much less carry on any type of normal life.

The week before Christmas of 2007 is still a blurry mass of days that seem like someone else's life. Yet, it was in that week that we learned a new lesson in the grace of God. We learned that no one is immune to the pains and tragedies of life. God never promised us a life free of suffering. He did promise that we would never suffer alone. People have often misunderstood what the biblical writers had to say about suffering. Commonly, people say, "the Bible says God will not put more on you than you can handle." That is simply not true. If we could handle it, we would not need His grace.

One of my favorite preachers, Bob Pitman, once delivered a message on the subject of burden bearing at a pastor's conference I was attending. He declared that God will allow more to come on you than you can handle. But, He will never allow more to come upon you than you and He can handle together. God's grace is his sustaining presence that sees us through the darkest storms of life.

I have learned a key ingredient to weathering a storm is that we must be careful not to give the storm too much credit. Letting the storm become bigger than our heavenly Father is the first step to succumbing to the onslaught. We become lost in the confusion and lose sight of the fact that His grace is sufficient even for such a time as we are suffering through. That is absolutely true regardless if the storm is cancer, a marriage in disarray, the loss of a loved one . . . the possibilities are as endless as His grace but none are more powerful.

The greatest life lesson that I have learned through my storm is the same lesson the apostle Paul learned as he cried out to the Lord. One morning, on my way to church, I was listening to the pre-race commentary regarding the weekly NASCAR race on sports radio. I heard one of the guys say at such and such time we will hear the four most exciting words ever spoken: "Gentlemen start your engines!" Well, those might be the most exciting words he has ever heard, but the most exciting four words I can think of are: His Grace is Sufficient!

The following appears in a list in the front of a journal I kept during my journey. I share this list only to demonstrate the grace and power of God.

- December 12—mass found under my tongue
- December 13—MRI
- December 14—Needle Biopsy
- December 15—Received word the mass was malignant
- December 17—Received word of the specific type malignancy
- December 18—Pop killed in an accident at work
- December 20—Funeral
- January 3—Extensive surgical biopsy at Vanderbilt
- January 15—Began chemo treatments

God's grace was sufficient for all that came our way. Oh, like Paul, we had prayed that it would not be cancer. It was. We had prayed it would be easily dealt with. It was not. I began to pour over the Psalms looking for comfort and some promise that I could claim for healing and long life. It was not there. I had come to a place beyond my ability to cope. I could not handle this storm. It was too big for me. Ironically, I discovered that is the perfect situation to experience the grace of God. Indeed, it is only when we get to the end of ourselves that we see God's amazing grace in action.

We began to refocus our prayers. We prayed for opportunity to grow in the Lord. We prayed for opportunity to minister to others. And, yes, we prayed for healing. Ultimately, the prayer for healing is the safest prayer a believer can pray. John declared in Rev. 21:4 that there will come a day where disease will have no more power. However, we must acknowledge that while in this life disease is powerful. Storms of tremendous magnitude do come and threaten our way of life.

Paul learned that God's grace is sufficient. He had known it was sufficient for salvation. But, he was to learn that God's grace is sufficient for living as well. In the context of the verses used to introduce this chapter, the Apostle Paul had called out to God on at least three occasions asking him to remove a thorn from his flesh. While many have speculated, we do not really know what Paul's "thorn in the flesh" was. We do know that it caused him great concern, great stress. Perhaps the identity of the thorn is not revealed so that it may be applied to whatever trouble you might be experiencing. Rest assured, God's grace is available, and it is sufficient.

Life can present you with some very difficult situations. God never promised our journey would be problem free. By His grace I stand today. Many people have shared with me that my faith through this period of time has been an inspiration to them. In reality, God's grace sustained me. I want to share an acrostic with you that I believe the Lord gave me about grace.

G-enerous (large, abundant, ample)

R-adical (totally different from the chaos of the world . . . saving, sustaining, glorifying)

A-biding (consistent, same yesterday and forever)

C-ompassion (grace flows from the love of God)

E-ndurance (the ability to bear pain, hardship, or adversity; comes from the root word *endure*; to bear patiently; tolerate; to suffer without yielding.)

Have you experienced God's amazing saving grace? If you have, embrace His grace that the power of Christ might be demonstrated in times of your afflictions.

CHAPTER 3

THE SEARCH FOR PEACE

**He who dwells in the shelter of the
Most High will abide in
the shadow of the Almighty.
I will say to the LORD,
"My refuge and my fortress,
My God, in whom I trust!"
Ps 91:1-2 (NAS)**

As stated in the previous chapter, at the beginning of my journey through cancer, I searched frantically for peace. My heart was heavy, and I was terrified. In fact, there are still days when fear creeps back in. I realize that is not very spiritual and not what you might expect to hear from a pastor. I have heard people say they had peace from the beginning or they were never afraid. I rejoice for them. Perhaps I did not have it because God had work to do in my life. Perhaps, at times, we are just not willing to admit our fears. I can say without embarrassment that

I was afraid. I have also found that I am not alone in that. Fear is innate. The psalmists experienced it as well as other great personalities in the Bible. Knowing great fear is the only way to know great peace.

Childhood memories can be wonderful things to look back on for life's lessons. I remember as a child going to spend a couple of weeks at a time in the summer with my aunt Zelma and uncle Carley. They lived in Mansfield, Tennessee, on a simple family farm. Three or four cows had to be milked by hand every day. The hogs had to be slopped. The slop was a gross concoction that began with dishwater, and I really do not remember what all else went into the recipe. The hogs seemed to love it, whatever it was. Of course, the garden had to be hoed and picked. Oh yes, the house had no indoor bathroom either. An outhouse stood several steps away with his and her sides. It was a wonderful adventure for a young boy!

One particular memory that sticks out in my mind really had no significance until much later in life. Yet, it has stuck with me all of these years. For some odd reason, I remember a day when a storm approached the little farm. The wind began to blow, and it got really dark. My aunt and uncle had free range chickens, which means they were not in a pen. They just wandered all over the place scratching, clucking, and doing other things chickens do. I really enjoyed playing with the little baby chicks. When this storm approached, I vividly remember these little chicks running like their lives depended upon it to the mother hen. They ran to her and she nestled down on them and covered them with her wings. They were completely safe and out of harm's way . . . even though the storm was still raging.

The lessons from this event of nature are many. The Bible says that the Lord wanted to do something similar for the Israelites. He said that He often wanted to gather them together as a hen does her chicks, but they would not allow Him to. The lesson I have learned, as the Lord has brought this childhood memory back to me once again, has been dramatic. I am not sure those little chicks were looking for safety . . . or a place of peace in the storm. They were simply looking for their mother. They could have run all over that farm and not found safety. But when they found their mother and the shelter of her wings, peace was complimentary.

I searched over a period of time for peace. I prayed for it. I read the Scriptures seeking it. I longed for it. I cried for it. I begged for it. I only found it when I ceased looking for it and just sought the Father. As I got closer to Him, peace was complimentary. It really was an amazing thing. I found several verses that helped me in this. One is under the glass top on my desk that I read almost daily. The passage is included at the beginning of this chapter but let us read them again. The Psalmist declared, "He who dwells in the shelter of the Most High will abide in the shadow of the Almighty. I will say to the Lord, 'my refuge and my fortress, My God whom I trust'" (Ps. 91.1-2)

That passage sounds very similar to the story of those little chicks. It is a good place to be, safely sheltered under the all powerful "wings" of the

Almighty who just happens to be my Heavenly Father. Find Him and you find peace. Look for peace and you may never find it.

One other note about peace: It is a gift. Jesus said in John 14:27, "Peace I leave with you; My peace I give to you; not as the world gives, do I give to you. Let not your heart be troubled, nor let it be fearful." (NAS)

CHAPTER 4

THE POWER OF PRAYER

After this manner therefore
pray ye: Our Father which art in
heaven, Hallowed be thy name.
Thy kingdom come.
Thy will be done in earth,
as it is in heaven.
Give us this day our daily bread.
And forgive us our debts,
as we forgive our debtors.
And lead us not into temptation,
but deliver us from evil:
For thine is the kingdom,
and the power,
and the glory,
forever. Amen.
Matt 6:9-13

Personal Prayer

In the months following my diagnosis, I learned more deeply the power of compassion . . . the preciousness of love . . . the calming of human touch....yet all of those wonderful things have limits in scope and effectiveness. One tool, or practice, at our disposal, however, has no limit. Prayer. The reason prayer is limitless in its power is because the One to whom we pray is limitless in power.

During those days following my diagnosis I began to pray earnestly for healing. When you are in the midst of a storm, do not be afraid or feel guilty about praying for yourself. It is not necessarily a selfish act. As we have seen, the apostle Paul prayed for his thorn to be removed. All through Scripture we see individuals praying for their own particular needs. As a child of God, I believe our Father wants nothing more than for his children to turn to him.

Let me be clear that I am not a proponent of the prosperity gospel that is prevalent today. I have prayed too often in faith, believing, and things not go the way I wanted them to. I have seen many godly people who were pillars of faith not have health or wealth, at least as the world would define it. I do, however, believe that God can do whatever He wants and that prayer does make a difference. Prayer certainly changes us.

In the first couple of weeks of my radiation and chemotherapy combination, I developed a severe infection requiring hospitalization. The doctor was very frank with me that the situation was serious. During that five day hospital stay, I received a book in the mail. I do not even know who sent it as I lost the letter that came with it. But, that little book changed my life. The title of the book was "Cancer and the Lord's Prayer." I will not try to share the contents of the book, but I do highly recommend it.

We were eleven weeks into the treatment phase and four months or so past my diagnosis. The next five weeks were going to be the most trying of all. The side effects would grow more intense. However, the loneliest time was a nine minute span when I lay on a steel table, with my head securely fastened to it with a mesh mask that appeared to be created for some horror film. There was an opening in the front. A tube was placed through the hole and into my mouth to hold my tongue in place while the radiation machine moved into position and delivered radiation to nine different entry points. We did this thirty-five times.

My mind wandered. For the first two weeks I cried secretly, every day, behind the mask. Then that little book came. I read it through the first time without putting it down. It gave me a new perspective on the Lord's Prayer. From that day on, as the wonderful attendant snapped my mask into place, I began to recite the Lord's Prayer. I would change things up and make it more personal. Phrases like "My Father" and "thy will be done on this table as it is in heaven" turned my tears of loneliness into times of worship. I cannot explain the peace that filled that room.

Prayers from Church Family

Our church has a tremendous prayer ministry. We pray and we send prayer cards for encouragement-not one card only, but everyone who prays fills out a card. I'm telling you, receiving an envelope or two of those things will lift a person's heart. Having received those cards I know the impact. They are simple yet moving. They are reminders of the power of prayer and the fact that people are praying.

I will never know all the people who prayed for me. Churches all over the United States and other parts of the world were praying. My church family (First Baptist Bemis) interceded on my behalf in a dramatic way. I use the following example not to leave others out but to demonstrate the impact of prayer.

One day I received an email that was not supposed to be forwarded to me. I sat at the computer and wept. Then as quickly as I could, I went to the window to look at the street in front of my house. You see, the email I got was from Beth, a lady in our church on whom God had planted a burden to do "drive by prayer." Her heart was simply to drive by my house while praying to the Father on my behalf! She had issued an invitation for others to join her.

I do not know how many people participated in the drive by prayer effort. I can tell you that every time I heard a car pass our house on that little side street in Watlington Woods, my spirit was lifted! It was a reminder that there were people, countless people, people I was not even aware of, praying for me.

Never underestimate the power of your prayers in the lives of hurting people. Prayer may be all you can do, but it is also the most powerful thing you can do!

CHAPTER 5

ONE MORE

**Look at the birds of the air; they
do not sow or reap or store away
in barns, and yet your heavenly
Father feeds them. Are you not
much more valuable than they?
Therefore, do not worry about
tomorrow, for tomorrow will
worry about itself.
(Mt. 6.26, 34ab)**

This is a short chapter but needed, simple yet profound. Please do not set it aside too quickly or just count it as cliché. One day at a time is truly the best approach to dealing with a storm.

Nine weeks of chemo followed by seven more weeks of chemo combined with thirty-five radiation treatments on my mouth and throat area was too much to digest and deal with at one time. Thinking about what was before me was too overwhelming to think of as one big unit. So, I broke it down to smaller portions I could handle. I decided I could do anything for one day. This may sound silly and simplistic, but it helped me, and that is what this book is about. I want to try to pass on what helped me and hope that it may help you or someone else.

My mindset was, not that I had sixteen chemo treatments, but that I had one chemo treatment sixteen times. I did not face thirty-five days of radiation; I faced one day of radiation. I just had to do that thirty-five times.

I went to high school with a guy who ran marathons. He would eventually run in the Boston marathon. I asked him one day, "How do you run twenty-six miles?" His response was something that I would be reminded of in a variety of life situations and certainly had impact on my cancer journey. He said, "I don't run twenty-six miles; I run one mile at a time." He told me that there are mile markers along the way. He would run from one mile marker to the next until there were no more mile markers. That was when the race was over.

There were many nights when sleeping was difficult. The pain, the mucus, the difficulty swallowing that would eventually become almost impossible, the emotional swings, the needle sticks, hospital stay, chemo treatments, radiation treatments, excruciating sores in my mouth, inability to eat or even want to eat, the choking, the weakness, burning, cream application, tears, and wondering, could all be broken down into a twenty-four hour period. I just had to get through the day at hand. Whatever that day had in store,

God's grace was sufficient. I would get through it and face tomorrow, tomorrow.

I also used this approach to help me to enjoy the day as well. No matter how difficult the day, there was always something to enjoy. Please hear this: don't miss living today worried about tomorrow. You may not have tomorrow, that is true for all of us, but you do have today. Do not waste it!

This one day at a time thing is very strange for me. You see, I have always been a worrier. I guess some would call that a lack of faith. However, we are all wired a bit different and worrying seems to be part of my DNA! My wife is one of those people who can just put things out of her mind. She is the least worrying person I know.

My mind is always on the next thing, the next day, way out in the future. Sometimes that is good; sometimes that is not so good. I imagined all the anguish I would go through before I ever got to that point. I imagined my boys without their dad and my wife without her husband. I wondered what would happen to them. I wandered through the house because I could not sit still. Those early days were filled with constant groaning in my spirit. At times, those groanings were audible. I was downcast much of the time.

I came to realize this was a time of grieving. I had walked this phase of life with many people before. I had experienced it with the death of my dad and other close loved ones. While this grieving had a much different cause, it was still just as much of a process. The valley of grief can be deep, but we must make sure it is not too long. I've seen people go into the valley of grief and never come out. In the case of the loss of a loved one, living life in the valley of grief does not bring them honor. They would want us to live. In the case of the storms of life, living in grief and worry gives the storm victory.

I decided that my family may have to watch me suffer through the treatment process. We had no choice in that. But the people around me didn't have to watch me die every day and that is what I was doing. I realized it was very selfish of me to rob them of, not only seeing joy in my life, but of any joy they may have as well. I determined to live "today" to the fullest. By God's grace, I would smell the flowers. I would enjoy the summer breezes and hear the singing birds. I would escape in the embrace of my wife. I would enjoy Matthew's ballgame. I would hear the music as it flowed from Scott's heart down his arms through his fingers and onto the piano keys. Today is a good day. Sure, some days are better than others. But we can make every day good.

This one-day-at-a-time way of living, allows us to endure the difficult days. We know that in twenty-four hours even the toughest day will be over. This mindset will also, and more importantly, allow us to live in the moment, enjoy the time, cherish the moment, and not "borrow trouble" as Gertrude used to say. She was my sweet grandmother.

Perhaps you are familiar with this hymn:

One day at a time, sweet Jesus,
That's all I'm asking from you.
Just give the strength
To do everyday what I have to do.
Yesterday's gone, sweet Jesus,
And tomorrow may never be mine.
So, help me today, show me the way,
One day at a time.
(Marijohn Wilkins/Kris
Kristofferson)

CHAPTER 6

ROUTE 66 LIVING

The flowers appear on the earth;
the time of the singing of
birds is come.
Song of Solomon 2.12

Travelers on land in this great country may get from one place to another one of two ways. One may take the quickest route, the interstate system. The interstate system was developed to handle a large volume of traffic traveling at a high rate of speed. By taking the fastest option, you will get where you are going, but the scenery is likely to be limited. Not that you will not witness some beautiful sights, but those who developed the fastest route did not do so with scenery as their primary goal.

Travelers may choose the scenic option as opposed to the faster route for their journey. You need to be aware of some very important features of the scenic route. Speed limits are usually much lower than the interstate. There will likely be more stops along the way. Progress will be hindered by having to travel through little towns along the way. Roadways are often two lanes that may have to be shared with a tractor or some other slow moving vehicle. The scenic route is usually the road less traveled because most people just want to get from point A to point B so that they can get on the task at hand and get back to point A and start all over again.

Route 66 was a famous scenic route across America. I have seen it portrayed in movies and read about it in books. The glory days of that great scenic drive have long been gone. I never got to experience it. A few sections still exist but most of Route 66 has been replaced by Interstate 40. I believe we have lost more than simply a piece of Americana. We have lost the ability and even joy of slowing down and enjoying the ride.

I must admit I lived my life primarily on the interstate rushing from one task to the other. One thing my storm caused me to do was to take notice and appreciate the little things that were always there, but I was missing them. I remember one day when I felt like sitting outside, I went out on the deck at the back of our house. A blue bird happened to visit that day, and as I looked at it, it seemed to be the most beautiful one I had ever seen. The colors were brilliant. It was alive with activity, doing blue bird things. I realized that day that I had missed a great deal of life rushing from one thing to the next.

While I enjoy traveling the scenic route from time to time, most of my automobile travel ends up being on the interstate. But I determined sometime ago that my way of living life was going to be more like that Route 66 travel than that of Interstate 40. I want to experience life! I want to pull over and smell the flowers. When a sign reveals a scenic overlook ahead I want to take time to pull over and gaze at the beauty of this great life.

Dottie and I enjoy riding our motorcycle. Travel is much different on a motorcycle than in a car, even beyond the obvious. The sights, sounds, and even smells are often quite extraordinary. On one occasion, we went for a short ride and I just noticed all the smells. As we rode out through the country, I smelled fresh cut grass and honeysuckle. We rode back into town past the restaurants. The delicious aroma of all of the food being cooked was alluring. I want to experience life that way, and I challenge you to do the same.

We particularly enjoy riding the Natchez Trace Parkway. The trace extends from near Nashville, Tennessee, to Natchez, Mississippi. We have ridden the entire route a few times, but our favorite section is between Tupelo and Jackson, Mississippi. The speed limit is 45 miles per hour and there is no commercial traffic. All along the way we are free to stop and read the many historical markers or take the short hikes along trails to scenic overlooks. We might even walk the boardwalk through a portion of a swamp. We might see dozens of turkeys scratching for food or a doe grazing with her fawn. Our pace is slow, and our goal is simple. Relax and enjoy the ride. Not a bad approach to daily life, huh?

I picked up a book the other day, and the title caught my attention. The title? Good Sermons for Great Days. I immediately thought, "I need a book titled 'Great Sermons for Good Days.'" I have come to believe that every day may not be great, but every day is good. I want to be sensitive to every moment. I do not want to miss a moment of life by rushing past it or having my senses clouded by worry.

Ours is truly a world of the instant. Instant information, instant messaging, instant news, instant coffee, and I am sure if we could we would do instant travel. But, think of all that we would miss. Much of humanity is moving from one task to another paying little or no attention to the beauty and opportunities around them.

Those of us who have weathered the storm have a unique opportunity that the rest of the world may not have learned. We can understand the significance of the moment and embrace the opportunity to enjoy each precious view, smell, touch, sound, and experience. I want to walk my life much more slowly!

CHAPTER 7

GOD IN SKIN

A very present help in trouble.
Psalm 4.15.36

On any journey we encounter many people. Most have no major impact. They are simply people in passing. We stand in line with them in a restaurant or pass by them at a rest stop. Perhaps we sit or stand with them on an amusement ride or sit near them on the beach. Sometimes we meet individuals who provide some lasting influence in our lives. These people impact our lives in such a way that we cannot imagine our lives without their influence. When we journey through a storm, we often come face to face with some incredible people. Or, we gain new insight and appreciation for people we have known a long time.

The following is a representation of those who made a huge difference in my journey. I know and acknowledge that I will leave out names of many individuals who helped me and ministered to me during those most difficult days. I prayerfully request that each and every person who prayed for me and assisted in any way during my journey will accept those mentioned below as a representation of all who took part.

Space will not allow me to put into words my love and thankfulness for my family. I know the journey was difficult for them. The storm was fierce and destructive on those who love me the most. I want to say a word or two about my dear wife. Dottie was nominated for and received the Katherine Bond Caregiver Award at our annual Madison County Relay for Life Event. (Relay for Life is an event that raises millions of dollars for cancer research. I must take this opportunity to encourage you to join a team or start a team. It's fun! Call your local American Cancer Society for more information) Now, back to my wife. She is the most caring person I have ever known. She really took that "in sickness and in health" vow seriously. When I was not a good patient, she demonstrated patience. When I wanted to quit, she spurred me on. When I was not very lovable, she loved me anyway. When I did not have the strength to walk, she was my crutch. When it was the darkest, God shined His light through her.

Many who ministered to us in our moment of need may not even be aware of it. Their impact in our lives may have been dramatic and brief at the same time. We may or may not even know their names. Or, we might just know their first name from the tag clipped to their clothing. Such is the case with Dennis. I do not even know what Dennis' official position is at the Henry B. Joyce Cancer Clinic at Vanderbilt Medical Center. I have seen him doing a number of things.

It was January 11, 2008, and my first visit to the clinic. We were on our way to meet Dr. Jill Gilbert who would be my oncologist. I did not know it at the time, but she would become my friend and, next to Dottie, my head cheerleader. Dottie had been in a meeting near Nashville, and Scott, along with Laurel, a family friend, drove me to meet her, so that we could go to the appointment together. After meeting Dottie, we made the mad dash to find the clinic. Naturally, we were running late and were not really sure where we were going. In a rush we exited a hallway and rounded a corner and there it was! We stood, me frozen in my tracks, in front of a sign that read Henry-Joyce Cancer Clinic.

I have visited hospitals regularly over the years of my ministry. I have celebrated the birth of children and walked through the valley of the shadow of death with families. High times and low times, times of good news and times of devastating news have all been part of my experiences in hospitals. We have all been in those types of situations.

But this time was different. Numbness is the best way to describe how I felt. Surreal is the only word that comes to mind for that moment. I knew I was walking into the clinic, but it seemed as though I was there for someone else. When I saw the sign, I almost went to my knees. This was a cancer clinic. I was here not for someone else but for me. The reality of having cancer was still settling in. I had prayed before we got out of the car in the parking garage that God would make my steps strong. So, I gripped Dottie's hand, she gripped mine, and we walked in.

I do not even know if Dennis spoke to me that day. But there he was. His face was glowing with a brilliant and compassionate smile. As I watched him interacting with other patients, my ridged tension filled body began to relax. Breathing became more normal. God used Dennis that day to calm me. In fact, it would be the first step in my feeling at home in that place. That may sound silly and may be silly, but rather than a scary place, the Henry B. Joyce Cancer Clinic and Vanderbilt Medical Center have become places of refuge and encouragement.

I was about to meet one of the most vibrant women I had ever met. Her voice filled the waiting room every time she called out, "patient holding pager number forty-nine," or whatever the number might have been. Her call was for the pager holder to come to the adjoining lab for blood work. I was a number that day but it would be the last day I felt like a number. Victoria made the process of having blood drawn seem like some sort of party. She remains a joy every time I see her. But on that first day, I noticed on the dry erase board this phrase, "Have a blessed day." You know, that day was turning out to be better than I had imagined. Dennis and Victoria, just going about their work, were ministering angels to me that day, and I am not even sure they knew it. I do not even know their last names.

We also met Rita that first day in the clinic. Rita was responsible for talking to new patients about clinical trials. I seem to recall that Rita had been involved in oncology as a nurse for forty years or so and had retired a couple of times already. Well, she was out of retirement again and was there for me that January day. While we opted for a more traditional course of treatment, we developed a bond that day that remains. Her caring eyes, her soothing voice, and loving presence will always be remembered. Over time we have cried together and laughed together. When she finds out we are there for a visit, she looks us up and hugs us two or three times. She would later tell one of our friends who had accompanied me to a treatment that I had touched her heart. I do not know about that, but I do know that she touched ours.

Let me just say, every nurse I have had the privilege of encountering has been a wonderful blessing. They have all been caring and compassionate. I cannot imagine having traveled this journey without them. But, there was only one first nurse in regard to my chemotherapy treatments. The day I walked into Vanderbilt for my first chemotherapy treatment was much like that first day at the cancer clinic, it was surreal. This day was also scary. It was surreal because once again it seemed like it was someone else going through this ordeal. I mean, I really couldn't have cancer. But I did. It was scary because it was all new and unknown.

Sitting in the waiting area, I was surrounded by people like me. There were young and not so young, men and women, all with the same hope and plan: get well. Some had lost their hair. Some looked nervous. Others flipped through magazines or read books. All were facing a deadly disease and the battle of their lives. I was just trying to take it all in and at the same time just get through the day.

Vanderbilt has a new chemo lab now and I have visited the nurses there a number of times. The old lab is where I had all of my treatments. The main area consisted of a large room where the nurses' station filled the center. Around the perimeter of the room were small cubicles with a chemo chair and a chair for caregivers. I spent my time watching Scooby Doo on the small television between naps. I took a book or magazine to read but was never able to concentrate enough to read the first page. Scooby Doo watching takes very little concentration!

Anyway, that first day, January 15, 2008, as I walked into the chemo lab and took my seat in the chemo chair, I met Billie. I cannot describe the feelings that were going through my mind as I sat down. But, I can tell you that Billie, my first chemo nurse, the one who would insert the needle in my arm and start the medicines that would attack my cancer, was wonderful. She was kind, sweet, informative, and gentle. She explained the process although I could not tell you a thing she said. She helped Dottie know what to expect. She prepared my pre-meds and got me "hooked up" to the IV. She put in a DVD for me to watch, but informed me that I would not remember any of it due to my pre-meds. She was right. Those meds always made me loopy.

I told Billie that I wanted to know when the pre-meds were finished and when she was starting the first of the two chemo drugs I would be getting. As I looked up at the plastic bag hanging on the IV pole and saw the first drop of Taxol drip from the bag into the line, I said to it, "Go get that cancer!" Billie sat down beside my chair and watched me. I know she was watching for any side effects so that she could intervene quickly, but, in the few moments we had known each other, she had become my friend. I was just glad to have a friend there with us. God used her to bring a period of calm in the storm.

I remember looking over at Dottie, as I would on a number of occasions, and feeling so broken hearted and sorry for her. It hurt me to see her hurting. It scared me to think of her watching me suffer and face the possibility of watching the cancer take its ultimate toll. She is strong and God has given her grace. She has passed that grace along to me through the whole process.

I hope that if you have to go through what I have gone through you have a Fulton Mullis in your life. I call him Brother Fulton because he is a senior member of our church and a deacon. I have great respect for him. But he is more than a fellow church member. He has been a blessing to our family beyond explanation. He is my friend. He has done handyman work at our house, been a confidant and encourager beyond explanation. We have laughed together and cried together. When the cancer word came was a time we cried together.

Bro. Fulton accompanied me on numerous visits to the doctor. He sat with me at home. One day sticks out in my mind beyond all others. Dottie was in Columbia, Tennessee, for training regarding her job and could not go to my chemo treatment. I was nervous about her not being with me. But, once again, God in skin came along. Brother Fulton is a kind, gentle servant. He genuinely counted it a joy to go with me, and it sure was a joy for me. We ate at the Cracker Barrel, his favorite restaurant, I believe. Or, maybe we ate in the food court that day. We did one or the other on occasion.

As we made our way around my stops from lab work to the chemo chair, he was amazed. There was constant activity. When the pre-meds began, Brother Fulton became more to me than words can ever express. What I am sharing with you now could be embarrassing, but it is just humbling and describes what I mean by God in skin. The pre-meds made me really unstable on my feet, almost high every time. This day, however, the effects were more severe than usual. Fortunately, the only real task for me to carry out was going to the restroom.

Due to the amount of fluids being pumped into my body, I needed to go the restroom every fifteen minutes or so. This was an especially difficult day for some reason. I informed Brother Fulton I had to go to the restroom, which was across that big room. He helped me up and followed closely behind me as I used my IV pole for stability. He then helped me to get into the restroom. He then turned his back to me and stood facing the corner until I was ready to return to my chemo-bed.

It has been more than two years since that day and I am writing this with tears in my eyes. We repeated the process seven or eight times on that day. He would help me up, follow me to the restroom, help me back into the bed, cover me up, put pillows behind my head, adjust the TV, and jump up every time I moved. We were gone from home eleven hours that day. He would end up being my travel partner and helper on many occasions. Fulton Mullis is a blessing!

I want to get very personal at this point. Speaking in generalities is usually not a good approach. However, we guys are not so good at letting people help us. For some reason, we generally operate with an "I can handle this myself" attitude. We consider it a sign of weakness if we depend on support from someone else. But let me tell you something very important. When the storm begins, being secure enough to allow yourself to be helped along the way is vital to you and to those around you.

God has gifted some of them with a tremendous spirit and heart to reach out. When we refuse to allow them to help, we rob them of opportunities to use their gifts and, in effect, reject the care that God is offering us through them. As I look back over my journey, some of my most embarrassing moments were spent with Brother Fulton by my side. Well, looking back, it is not embarrassing at all.

I could write about countless people, but I am going to close this chapter by mentioning a true hero to many people, and she was to me. Virginia Askew battled cancer for more than ten years. She and her husband, Richard, made numerous trips to M.D. Anderson in Houston. She loved the Lord, was a prayer warrior, Bible teacher, and encourager to everyone who knew her. I have many cards and notes of encouragement from Mrs. Virginia. But I want to share the one thing she said that helped me on my journey more than anything else. I share this hoping it will be an encouragement to you during the storms of life.

"Don't leave the blessings in the valley."

Mrs. Virginia was reminding me that even in the valleys there are great blessings to be had. If we are not careful, we will miss them. I challenge you not to leave the blessings in the valley! Thank you Mrs. Virginia.

I would never consider myself to be God in skin. However, I do believe that the things we endure, the battles we face, and the victories we win are to be used to the benefit of others. We can wallow in our pain. We can push past storms back into a vault deep inside of ourselves never to be considered again. We may even become bitter about the storm. I believe that doing either will actually allow the storm to continue to wield its power and cause clouds to reappear from time to time. Another option is to use your storm experience to help someone else suffering through a storm in their own lives.

The latter is what I have chosen to do. I am not saying I am doing a good job of it. But, I can say that doing what I can to offer encouragement and hope to others has continued to rob my storm of its power. It is the difference in being a victim and a victor. By giving back in some way, I have realized that I did not go through all I went through just for me. I have had the privilege to meet and walk with some incredible people. Hopefully, in some small way, I could be for someone what those mentioned above, and many others, were for me. I would encourage you to do the same. Look for ways to invest your experience into the lives of others. It truly will change your perspective on your storm.

CHAPTER 8

IT'S OK

**My heart races, my strength leaves
me, and even the light of my
eyes has faded.
Psalm 38.10**

It's ok to be afraid.
It's ok to cry.
It's ok to ask God questions.
It's ok to be concerned about the future.
It's ok to ask for help . . . it is ok to need others.
It's ok for you to take time to get better.
It's ok to dream and look forward to better days.
It's ok to plan for the future.

I mention this list of "it's ok's" because I had to learn my lessons the hard way concerning them. Storms are frightening events. Those who have never been through a storm do not understand. They cannot. I have learned that our storm identification process is not very good. As I look back over my life, knowing what I know now, I realize that I classified some events in my life, some seasons of my life, as storms when they were no more than a light breeze.

I have been accused of not demonstrating faith through my storm. That accusation came from one person yet it rang loudly in my ears. I allowed it to affect me greatly. I allowed her voice to drown out the countless voices that shouted otherwise. One day I finally came to the point when I understood that she had never had cancer, radiation, or chemo, and I would no longer give her permission to occupy that space in my mind.

People may say some hurtful things. They may mean to say them, or say them out of ignorance. In fact, you may get negative influences from any number of sources. In order to fight through the storm, you must dismiss them. They will rob you of needed power and strength, hinder your health, and steal the joy of living "today." You have the power to let them do it or to dismiss them. I challenge you to dismiss them and fight on!

As I mentioned before, upon my diagnosis I began to search the Scriptures for some promise I would be healed and live a long life. I did not find that. Certain people proclaim regularly that those promises exist, but I would challenge them to show me those verses in context and make their point. From what I see in scripture and what I observe in life, no one is immune to storms and no one is exempt from death.

I did find many examples in the Psalms alone that verify the statements made at the beginning of this chapter. The psalmists consistently demonstrated the same feelings that I have mentioned. I have come to realize that if we never experienced fear, we would never know the shelter of God's wings! We would never experience the overwhelming peace He provides in the midst of chaos. We must remember, in our weakness He is strong.

I could include a number of the Psalms, or portions of them, at this point. The problem is that I do not know which ones might speak to you the most. I do, however, believe God will speak to you through them. So, why not put this little book down for a time and pick up the Book of all books and read for yourself. Immerse yourself in the Psalms and experience the closeness of God and the power of His Word.

I will close this chapter with two verses from the Psalms that God has imprinted on my heart. I have already used them twice in this book. They are the first two verses of the 91st Psalm: "He who dwells in the shelter of the Most High will abide in the shadow of the Almighty. I will say to the Lord, 'My refuge and my fortress, my God in whom I trust.'"

CHAPTER 9

MY NEW NORMAL

**But one thing I do. Forgetting
what is behind and straining
toward what is ahead.
Phil. 3.14**

Intense spasms in my neck which are so painful at times I have to pull over in the car, or go to another room, or simply wait for it to subside, the left side of my tongue not functioning properly, dry mouth, dental issues, CT scans, throat scopes, fatigue, stiffness in my neck, concern over every little and not so little pain in my body, the awful noises I make to begin every day just to get my throat cleared and operational from my not so good night of sleep, and not being able to taste cakes, pies, and cookies may all seem like terrible reminders of the cancer or its treatment. But in reality, all of these side effects are reminders that I am alive!

Sure at times I still feel sorry for myself. Sometimes I wonder what my life would have been like if I had not had cancer. At times, it all still seems like a bad dream. But it is what it is. If I live in the "what ifs" and the "what was" of life then I will surely miss the here and now of life. The greatest tragedy of cancer would be for me to allow it to rob me of life while I am still living.

We have all received news that changed our lives forever. The word yes in response to "the question." "We're going to have a baby" certainly changes things. Receiving the news that I had cancer changed my life forever as did the treatment regimen. I suppose anyone treated for this disease, whether surgically or with radiation or chemotherapy or other treatment options, is never the same. Our bodies have been put through a lot in attacking this disease. Chemicals and objects, foreign to the human body, have invaded our bodies. Treatments are not without their side effects. So we all have a new normal, physically and emotionally.

People say and ask some strange things. At least they are strange to the ears of a storm survivor. One of my favorites is, "You look much better than the last time I say you." They ask some well-meaning questions that are motivated from genuine concern. Typically people ask, "How are you doing?" Even that question is a constant reminder that you have not been so well at one time.

As to the question, "How are you?" Sometimes I wonder. Sometimes I don't really know. That question can cover a lot of areas: emotionally, mentally, physically, and/or spiritually. At any given time, one or more of those areas are not like I would like them to be. But, the most difficult question is, "Are you back to normal?" I have come to learn that I am not "back" to normal, if that means like I used to be. But I have reached my "new" normal. The changes are reminders (I could have said difficulties, discomforts, etc.) but they are just reminders, periodic anxieties.

I wish I could say that there are no longer any clouds and the storm is completely gone and there is complete peace. But, there are times when I am reminded of the storm. Periodically I wonder if the cancer will return. If I am going to be completely honest, there are times I still feel sorry for myself. I wonder what my life might have been like without the storm. The trouble is, wondering such a thing is an exercise in futility. It is no different than going out after a devastating hurricane and imagining that it never came.

I can be a cancer victim or a cancer victor. The choice was largely up to me. The same is true for whatever storm you may face. You can be a victim of it or a victor over it. Sure, there are things I have to deal with every day that I never had to before as mentioned above.

I could go on but I really want to focus on the positive things that have become part of my new normal. I love my life! I have a wonderful wife and two great sons. I get to pastor a great church, preach God's Word, rely on His grace, and get up each day to a new adventure. I have been afforded the opportunity to encourage a number of people beginning a similar journey as mine. Each day is truly worth living. The list below is my "top ten" list. I am not even going to expound on them so that I might not influence you as you ponder on them and how they might apply to your life. Or, perhaps, and I would imagine you would, you will develop your own list.

1. Appreciation of just how precious life is.
2. Life is a journey; enjoy it!
3. Don't sweat the small stuff and most things are small.
4. Make the most of opportunities.
5. Be genuinely grateful for the most important things.
6. Keep a short list of non-negotiables.
7. Smile more; complain less.
8. Intentionally encourage others.
9. Walk slowly; don't miss a thing.
10. Think less about what might have been and more about what can be!

CHAPTER 10

RANDOM THOUGHTS

Finally, my brothers, rejoice in the Lord! It is no trouble for me to write the same things to you again, and it is a safeguard for you. (Phil. 3.1)

I would like to leave you with some closing thoughts, some takeaways if you will.

- Remember to live today.

A friend of mine once told me that his doctor reminded him to live today. That seems to be pretty good advice to me. I recently watch Jimmy Valvano's ESPY award speech from 1993. Valvano said that we should do three things every day: laugh, think, have our emotions moved to tears. He said, "if you laugh, you think, and you cry [from joy or sadness], that's a full day. That's a heck of a day."

- Today is the most important day.

As I lay in the my hospital bed in Jackson Madison County General Hospital with a mysterious infection, I believe the Lord placed the following thought in my mind: My life is in Christ and cancer cannot touch Him; therefore it can not touch my life. It can and has touched my body but it cannot stop my living! The words came to me just like that. Great peace flooded my heart and filled that room. It truly was one of those wow moments.

Jimmy Valvano's declared, "I don't know how much time I have left and I have some things I'd like to say." None of us really know how much time we have. We know that we have today. We should make the most of it.

- Smell the flowers

Whatever you do, savor the world around you. We truly live on a beautiful planet, filled with beautiful things and beautiful people. It would be a shame if we miss it all in our rush or worry.

- Open your eyes

We must not let the storm distort our vision. We must keep our eyes open to opportunities all around us to make a difference, to focus on others, and to realize we can find purpose even in the midst of a storm and especially after one.

- Remember this too will pass

You have heard all the clichés. It is always darkest before the dawn. Every cloud has a silver lining. Well, those are trite and may work for momentary discomforts. However, quaint little sayings provide little relief in the midst of a chaotic storm. But, as I said in the beginning, storms by their nature cannot last forever. We must simply press on. Take those treatments one at a time. Take those days one at a time. And, before you know it, the treatments will be over. Clouds will lift. Warm breezes will blow. The sun will shine.

- Let other people do what they can.

You do not have to journey alone. People who care will want to help. They find value and comfort in giving. Do not rob yourself or them of the great gift of helping you along the way. Whatever your storm, someone else has been where you are and they want to help. Others simply love and care about you and want to do something. It helps them cope with the storm which they endured. They may be suffering too. Let them do what they can.

- Encourage someone along the way.

As we journey through our storms we encounter a number of hurting souls along the way. People all around us stand in need of encouragement. Think of the opportunities. Nurses, doctors, people in the waiting room, the person in the next chemo chair, the possibilities are endless.

- There is life after diagnosis! Live it! (Enough said.)

CHAPTER 11

NO ONE JOURNEYS ALONE

**A chord of three strands is not
easily broken.
Ecclesiastes 4.12**

This closing chapter is dedicated to sharing a ministry that has grown out of my journey with cancer and into my new normal. As I said earlier, we can use the things we have gone through to assist and encourage others who might be going through similar storms of their own. While every storm is different and every person responds differently to the storm, we can help each other.

I hope you have not missed the term "journey" scattered throughout this book. From the moment I heard the word cancer, while sitting there on the steps just outside the worship center in First Baptist Church, Bemis until this very day, I have been on a journey.

I have learned some important lessons on this journey. I have learned some lessons from experience. Some lessons, I learned from others. One thing has become vital to my new normal and living life to its fullest. I believe I have a responsibility not to keep what I have learned to myself. Far too many people have heard the devastating news that they have cancer. They begin a journey that will be a difficult one.

My wife and I work with the American Cancer Society and our local Relay for Life, and we encourage you to do the same. We all need to promote ACS, which raises millions of dollars for cancer research. We desperately need more funds for research to fight this horrible disease.

To further give back, we have developed a ministry, Survivor2Survivor (S2S), dedicated to the goal that no one journeys alone. We want to shout from the rooftops that there is life after diagnosis and we want to help people experience it.

With S2S our simple goal is to make it possible for a cancer patient, in the midst of the journey, to have someone to call, email, or perhaps even visit face to face. Someone who understands. Someone who has been where they are. The concept may seem like a simple thing, and I suppose it is. But, for the one who needs the encouragement, the answer to a question, the calming interaction with someone who had a similar diagnosis and treatment, it is anything but simple.

Perhaps you have been given this book because you were recently diagnosed or you purchased this book at a seminar, and your purchase helped to support our ministry. Regardless the way you have received this book, we hope it will be a blessing to you and promote our cause.

From the time of my diagnosis, the medical caregivers went to work on the disease. But I was filled with fear, questions, concerns, etc., and there was no one for me to really talk to. I bugged my physicians to death. Friends told me about people they knew had been through something similar. I made the calls. S2S will provide a structured resource for the patients.

Strides have been made in the treatment of this horrible disease. Teams of medical professionals will go to work battling the disease in the bodies of those newly diagnosed people with all that science has to offer. We are thankful for these well trained, caring, and gifted people.

There is, however, a gap in the treatment of the whole person that we are seeking to fill. Upon diagnosis, the cancer patient begins taking steps, under the guidance of their medical caregivers, to deal with the physical aspects of their disease. From the initial word, through the treatment process, to their new normal, the patient's journey is an emotional rollercoaster to say the least.

Fear, anxiety, discouragement, disappointment, loneliness, despair, etc. are emotions the patient battles with. Patients may wonder what they can expect from a patient's perspective as they face treatments, side effects, recovery, and the future. Sometimes they just want to talk to someone who understands. This emotional battle can greatly affect their journey even while getting the best medical treatment available.

We stand ready to come along side cancer patients to help with the emotional side of the battle. S2S is a network of trained cancer survivors who link arms with healthcare providers and offer their hands, hearts, and ears to cancer patients who are either entering, or currently in, treatment of their disease. We seek to provide one on one support as the patient accepts and adjusts to the new reality they are faced with. Support is offered through a "Journey Partner" with similar diagnosis and treatment regimen to that of the patient. We claim no expertise, but we have been there. Our purpose is to provide hope, answer the questions we can, listen much, talk less, and help with coping skills during the journey.

Our primary message is: There is life after diagnosis.

Our primary goal is: No one journeys alone.

Our primary mission is: To provide a network of trained journey partners made up of cancer survivors to be a resource for newly diagnosed cancer patients.

*If you need our assistance please contact us. We want to hear from you.

*Some of you would be able to greatly assist our program in a very important way. The reality of the situation is that what we do incurs expense. The West Tennessee Healthcare Foundation has come along side us as the charity that manages our fund. You can give your tax deductible donation to our fund through them. WTHF does not have any control over the way we carry out our ministry; we determine how we function. WTHF is our partner in that they have accepted S2S as a fund in the foundation. We are very grateful to them for this great service.

For all types of correspondence email us at:
mark.survivor2survivor@gmail.com

* Should you wish to partner with us financially with your tax deductible gift, you may mail your donation to: WTHF
620 Skyline Dr.
Jackson, TN 38301-3923

Make sure to include: S2S Fund in the memo section of your check.

West Tennessee
Healthcare Foundation

An affiliate of West Tennessee Healthcare